Guide to the Constellations

by Susan Jones Leeming

PEARSON
Scott
Foresman

What You Already Know

Our Sun is really a star. It is the star that is closest to Earth. That is why it seems so big and so bright. All living things on Earth depend on the Sun's heat and light.

Earth spins on its axis, an imaginary line through its center. Earth rotates, or spins around completely, once a day. This rotation makes night and day. When the part of Earth where you live faces the Sun, you have day. When it rotates away from the Sun, you have night.

Earth is tilted on its axis and moves around the Sun in an orbit. Earth takes one year to orbit the Sun. Earth's tilt and its orbit around the Sun causes the seasons.

The Moon moves in an orbit around Earth. It takes about four weeks. The Moon goes through different phases, or shapes, during its orbit. The Moon has craters, which were caused by huge rocks crashing into it.

The Earth and the Moon are just two bodies in our solar system. There are seven other planets, most of which have moons as well. They all rotate around the Sun, making up our solar system.

The hundreds of stars that you see far away in the night sky are suns too. People have always looked at these stars and imagined lines connecting them, making pictures. These pictures are called constellations.

Stories of the Ancients

Ancient people looked up at the night sky and saw pictures. They imagined lines connecting the stars, making shapes called constellations. They gave these constellations names and told stories about them. The stories were about strange animals, heroes, and adventures. These stories were passed down to us.

We can still see the pictures the ancients saw in the night sky. They are many, many miles away from each other, and we know the stars in constellations do not have lines between them.

There are about eighty-eight constellations. Some are made of many stars. Others are made of only a few. Different constellations appear in the skies of the Northern and the Southern Hemispheres.

Stargazing

You can look at the stars in the sky and study them using star maps. Some star maps are on a wheel. You can spin the wheel to the right place and season. This round star map is called a planisphere. Once you have found the correct location on the map, you are ready to begin stargazing.

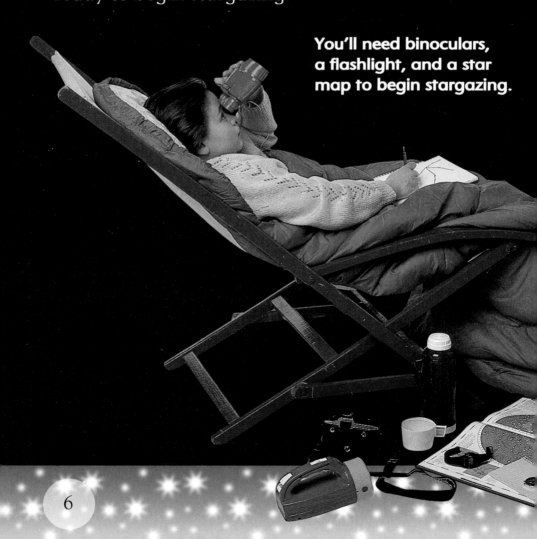

You'll need binoculars, a flashlight, and a star map to begin stargazing.

Ask a parent to take you to a place away from bright lights. Let your eyes get used to the darkness. Lie down and look up. Using a flashlight, compare what you see in the sky to what you see on your planisphere. Which constellations did you find? Which ones are still hiding from you?

Some star maps are printed on a wheel called a planisphere.

Zodiac Constellations

There are twelve constellations that can be seen from both the Northern and Southern Hemispheres. They are called the zodiac constellations. Each constellation appears in the night sky for about one month. Some people believe ancient farmers may have used the zodiac constellations as a calendar. When the spring constellations appeared, farmers knew it would soon be time to plant their crops. When the fall constellations appeared, they knew it was time to harvest.

People who lived thousands of years ago named the zodiac constellations. Different ancient people from around the world all told different stories about them. Some of the stories best known to us come from the ancient Greeks and Romans.

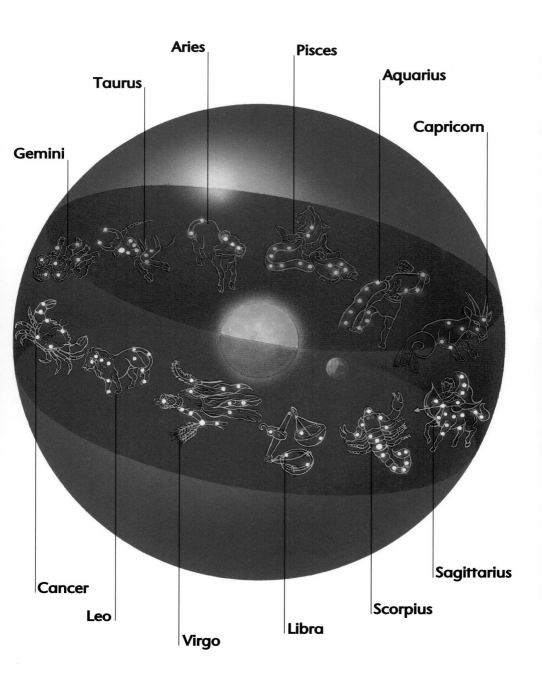

Gemini

Taurus

Aries

Pisces

Aquarius

Capricorn

Cancer

Leo

Virgo

Libra

Scorpius

Sagittarius

Cancer

The ancient Greeks told stories about pictures they saw in the night sky. One of their stories was about a hero named Hercules. He was half man and half god. Hercules was brave and had many adventures. Once he had to fight a monster named Hydra. A giant crab came to help Hydra fight Hercules. Hercules killed the crab and beat Hydra. Ancient Greeks named the six-star constellation after the crab. They called it Cancer.

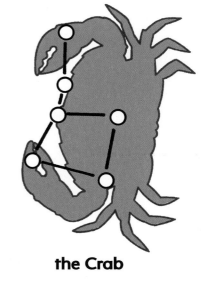

the Crab

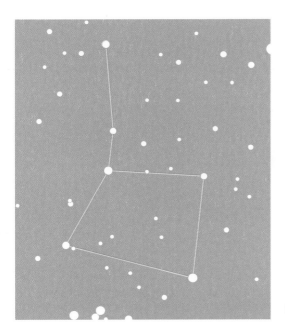

Cancer

Gemini

The ancient Greeks told a story about the twins Castor and Pollux. They were the twin sons of the Greek god Zeus and a woman named Leda. One day Castor was killed. Pollux missed his brother very much. He asked his father to help him. Zeus put Castor and Pollux into the night sky. There the two brothers lived together again.

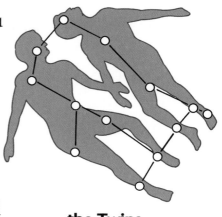

the Twins

Gemini

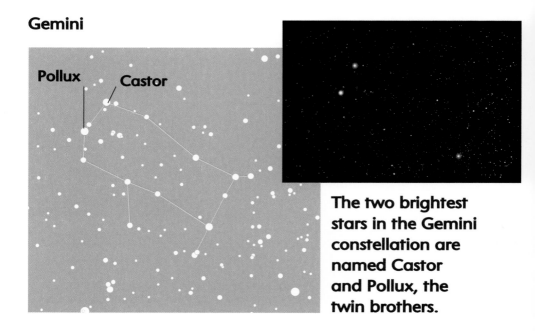

Pollux

Castor

The two brightest stars in the Gemini constellation are named Castor and Pollux, the twin brothers.

Leo

Every summer the ancient Greeks saw a lion in the sky. They called this lion Leo. Remember Hercules, the hero? The gods gave Hercules twelve jobs. His first job was to kill a dangerous lion. Afterward, Hercules always wore the lion's fur on his back.

the Lion

Can you see the picture of the lion in the stars below?

Leo

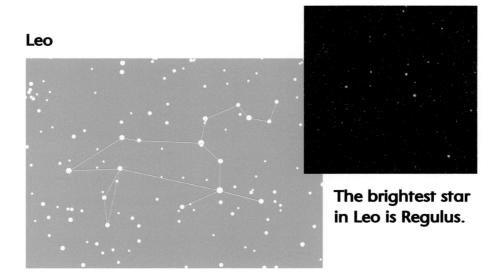

The brightest star in Leo is Regulus.

Libra

Libra is the only zodiac constellation that is not a person or an animal. Libra is in the shape of scales. Scales are tools used for measuring weight. An object is placed on one side and weights are placed on the other side until the two sides balance. The weights are counted to find out how heavy the object is.

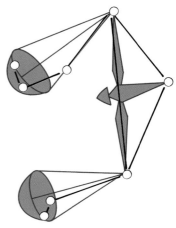

the Scales

The ancient Romans told stories about Libra. The scales made them think of fairness or equality because a scale can show equal weights.

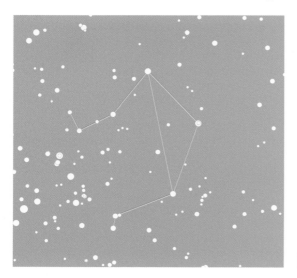

Libra

Scorpius

Scorpions are dangerous animals. Their poison is stored in their tail. If a scorpion stings a person with its tail, the person could die.

the Scorpion

The ancient Greeks did not see the scales in the stars of Libra. Instead they saw the claws of a scorpion. They named the constellation Scorpius. They told a story about the scorpion killing a brave hunter named Orion.

The people of Polynesia saw a fishing hook in the stars of Scorpius. Do you see Libra, a hook, or a scorpion in the picture below?

Scorpius

Taurus

The word Taurus means "bull" in Greek. The stars at the bull's back are named Pleiades. The stars at his nose are named Hyades. In the Greek story, the Pleiades and the Hyades are groups of sisters that ride on the bull. The bull protects the sisters from dangers in the sky.

the Bull

Look at the picture below. Can you find the sisters? Does the Taurus constellation look like a bull to you? Can it look like something else?

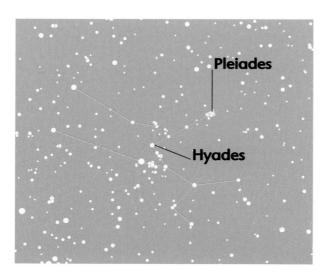

Pleiades

Hyades

Taurus

Other Constellations

There are many other constellations besides the twelve zodiac ones. Ancient people imagined stories about these other constellations too.

Andromeda

Andromeda was a beautiful Ethiopian princess. Perseus was a son of the god Zeus. He was on his way home from an adventure. He spotted beautiful Andromeda tied to a rock. A sea monster was about to eat her. Perseus killed the sea monster and saved the princess Andromeda. They fell in love and married each other.

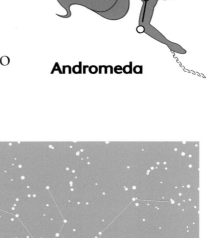

Andromeda

Andromeda

Cassiopeia

The W-shaped constellation is Cassiopeia. Cassiopeia and her husband, King Cepheus, were Andromeda's

Cassiopeia

parents. Cassiopeia bragged that she and her daughter were more beautiful than the sea nymphs. Poseidon, the god of the sea, heard this and became angry. He sent floods to kill Cepheus's kingdom. King Cepheus asked a wise man for help. The wise man told Cepheus that if he let a sea monster eat Andromeda, then Poseidon would not flood their land. Cepheus was going to do this, but Perseus rescued Andromeda from death!

Cassiopeia

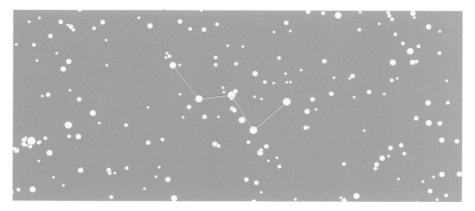

Canis Major

Canis means "dog" in Latin. Canis Major, or Greater Dog, was the dog of Orion, the brave hunter. Canis Minor, or Smaller Dog, was Canis Major's brother. Both dogs face other animal constellations in the sky. Canis Major faces Lepus, a rabbit-shaped constellation. Canis Minor faces Taurus, the bull. The ancient Greeks told stories about the two dogs chasing animals around the sky.

Canis Major

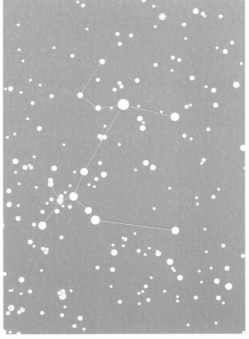

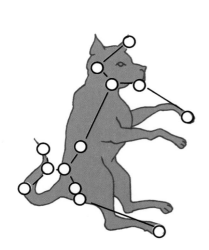

the Greater Dog

Crux

Crux is the Latin word for cross. The Crux constellation is also called the Southern Cross. This is because the Crux constellation is best seen from the Southern Hemisphere.

the Southern Cross

The stars that make up Crux are some of the brightest in the sky. Explorers have used Crux to help them sail across the sea. The bottom star points almost straight south.

Crux

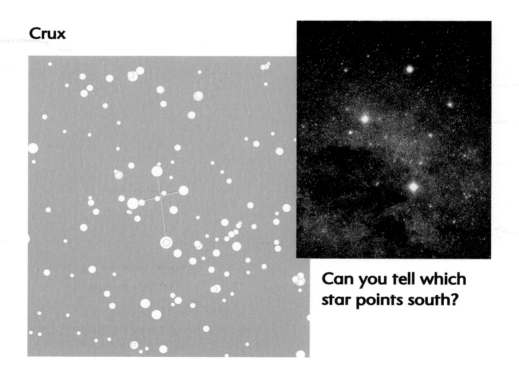

Can you tell which star points south?

Orion

The constellation Orion was seen by many ancient people. Greeks, Romans, and Arabs all have stories about this hunter. He hunted animals like Taurus, the bull, and Lepus, the rabbit, with his dogs. Orion's life ended when he stepped on a scorpion. The gods put Orion in the sky with his dogs and many animals to hunt. They put the scorpion far away from him!

the Hunter

Orion

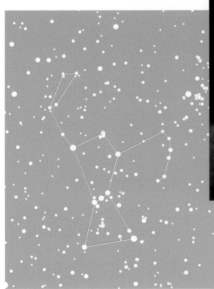

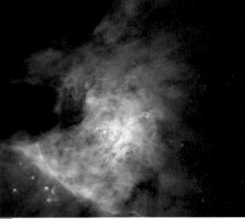

The star in the center of Orion's sword is a nebula— a huge gas formation where stars are born.

Pegasus

The ancient Greeks told the story of Pegasus. Pegasus is a flying horse. A brave son of the god Zeus killed a monster. Pegasus flew out of the

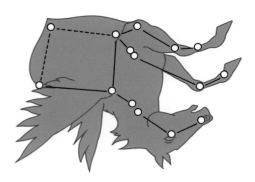

the Winged Horse

monster's neck. Even though the monster had been ugly and horrible, Pegasus was beautiful and good. Zeus, the king of all Greek gods, asked Pegasus to carry his lightning bolts.

Can you see the shape of a horse in the stars below? He is upside down! Can you imagine him running across the sky? What other pictures can you make with the stars of Pegasus?

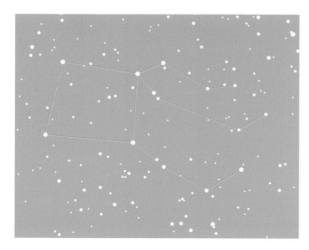

Pegasus

Ursa Major

Another animal Orion hunted is Ursa Major, the Great Bear. Ancient Greeks saw two bears in the sky, Ursa Major and Ursa Minor. Ursa Major is the big bear. Ursa Minor is the small bear.

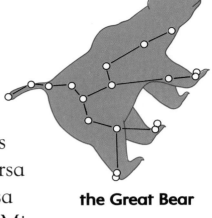

the Great Bear

Seven stars of Ursa Major make up another constellation called the Big Dipper. A dipper is a deep spoon or a ladle. Can you see the handle of the Big Dipper starting at Ursa Major's tail? Some people see the Big Dipper as a wagon, a plow, or warriors. What do you see?

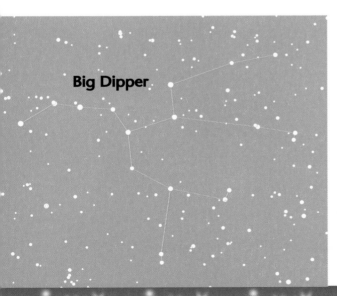

Big Dipper

Ursa Major

Do you see the Big Dipper or another picture in these stars?

What We Can See

Thousands of stars are visible in the sky. Over time people have seen many different pictures and shapes in these stars. All over the world people have used the stars to tell stories.

You too can make pictures with the stars in the night sky. You can make up your own stories, or you can look for the constellations you learned about. The next time you are outside at night, try stargazing!

Glossary

ancient   old, from the distant past

hemisphere   the top or bottom half of Earth

planisphere   a map of the stars

scale   a tool used to measure weight

stargazing   looking at and studying the stars

zodiac   the name for 12 constellations that can be seen from both the Northern and Southern Hemispheres